Nine Paths to Forgiveness

Understanding Ourselves and Others

By Chris Canfield

Drawings by Doug Meffert

Foreword by Tom Dodson

A Human Kindness Foundation Publication

Author: Chris Canfield

Drawings: Doug Meffert

Cover art: Keron McHugh, Head Artist & Owner,
The Cardinal Skin Art & Gallery, Mebane, NC

Foreword: Tom Dodson

Cover and book design by John Cotterman

Copies of this book are sent free to people in prisons and jails, and others who cannot afford to purchase a book. The Human Kindness Foundation is a non-profit organization which sponsors the Prison-Ashram Project and other programs promoting basic kindness and spiritual sanity. 100% of the proceeds from book sales and donations go to support these programs.

Human Kindness Foundation
PO Box 61619
Durham, NC 27715
humankindness.org

A Note From Sita Lozoff

For a long time I would hear an occasional conversation about the enneagram. I would only half listen, feeling that I really wasn't into learning something new--I already had my spiritual practices.

Then one day, Catherine invited me to her home to listen to a recording (she describes that at the end of this book). The first description I heard was number 8, and it was like hearing a clear and detailed description of someone who is dear to me. I couldn't believe how fully this speaker understood my friend! Since that day, I have used the Enneagram as part of my spiritual practice. I invite you to join me in that practice by studying this book.

A Note From Father Richard Rohr

After learning the Enneagram from my own Jesuit spiritual director in 1973, I have yet to find any other educational tool that so opens different groups of people to their own inner life. This might be especially true for the incarcerated who finally have the time and passion to know 'what makes them tick', as well as what makes everybody else tick in at least nine different ways! May *Nine Paths to Forgiveness* change your life in very helpful ways.

Foreword

by "Tall Tom" Dodson

I understand doing time! I did 34 calendar years collectively and 20 of that on my last sentence for armed robbery. Armed robbery was also what I went in for the first time when I was 22 years old.

I would talk to one of my homeboys or observe some other clown doing something, and I just "knew" they were off base and it wasn't going to work out. In the end I was off many times, but in each case I judged them as "messed up," or would say to myself "why can't they get this!?" Yet I was stubborn and failing to get it myself.

My yo-yo cycle of prison—being released, repeating the same or similar behavior, and returning to prison—finally forced me to look at life differently.

My spiritual path has included big doses of twelve-step recovery and many of the practices presented in Bo Lozoff's *We're All Doing Time*. These spiritual practices tend to direct our attention to predictable, patterned behavior that is unhealthy. They also speak about balance. For me balance sounded boring and bland. I craved the highest of highs or the lowest of lows. I liked to stir things up, even if the outcome was bad. I just wanted to change the way I felt, NO MATTER WHAT!

In spite of those cravings, I managed to get clean and sober. I got a daily spiritual practice. I got out of prison, found employment, served my community and found good friends. But I still had some deeply ingrained ways of thinking and acting. I was stubborn, and, as my sponsor said, "It seems like everything you ever let go of had claw marks on it."

So six years ago this vastly improved human being was frolicking around the planet when Sita Lozoff, co-founder with Bo of the Human Kindness Foundation, asked me to ride shotgun on a planned workshop in the Travis County Jail in Austin, Texas. During a series of preparatory phone conversations, Sita asked me if I was familiar with something called the enneagram.

In an effort to appear "worldly" I said "yes." The truth was I had quickly thumbed through one small book on the enneagram, learned nothing, yet my false pride had dismissed it as newspaper horoscope foolishness.

Sita pressed me further, revealing the limits of my knowledge. I made some vague promises to learn more about it, out of my respect for Sita, and promptly found reasons not to fulfill those promises. Then she called again. I didn't want to disappoint her, so I lied.

The truth was I found the whole enneagram thing—this system for understanding our personalities—overly complex. And I was probably afraid of what it might reveal about myself. I didn't know what to do. But the universe provided me a way.

I was searching for a small prayer book one day and happened upon the same book on the enneagram I'd tried to understand before. A second reading with an open mind changed my perspective. And then the universe just flooded me with opportunities: enneagram workshops, a twelve-step community that is interested in enneagram, and others. I came to understand my number: I am a seven.

I wish I could convey to you what a precious gift the enneagram has been to me. I am so enthusiastic about this puzzle piece in my life. I better understand my own motivations for acting or saying things in a particular way. It also gives me a deeper understanding of what motivates others. It allows me a new freedom that I really had no idea was available to me.

The understanding I've gotten from studying the enneagram gives me a more forgiving heart when I am faced with other people who are acting out in fear. In the past I would have labeled them an asshole or crazy. Both were judgments that I had often passed on myself. Even though I am often reminded of Ram Dass' saying, "I am that too"... I still would not really be in forgiveness because I was judging myself.

The enneagram is a tool I use to notice my ways of acting that are counterproductive. I can shift towards healthier responses that connect to my higher self. We are all aware that we all act differently, yet most of us look at others and say, "What is wrong with that guy, why can't he get this?"

The enneagram describes all of the billions of people on this planet in nine numbers. I challenge you to delve into this and disprove that. I know it sounds absurd, but so is being afraid of the internet, cellphones and restaurant menus. This simple tool allows us to better know each other and ourselves. Which in turn allows us to be more forgiving of ourselves and others.

I can look back on my prison experiences and see how they offered me the same men, the same correctional officers, hallways, locked doors and situations, over and over again. Those experiences began my spiritual transformation. I discovered that surrendering old ideas, beliefs and behaviors is the entrance to the path of peace.

I am grateful for Sita and all the friends who have helped me embrace and understand the simple yet powerful tool of the enneagram. We hope to be those friends for you. This book is designed to introduce the enneagram in hopes that you too can see and apply the benefits we have discovered, for the benefit of yourself and others.

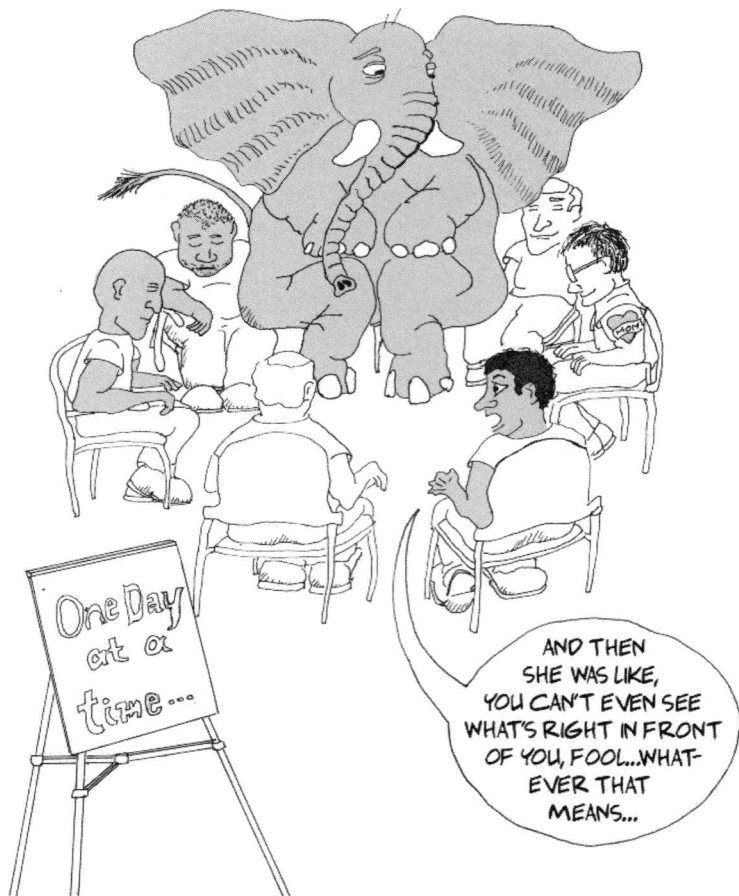

Walking the Path With The Enneagram

"The Enneagram works by a life-changing insight. It helps us to see our own compulsive blindness and how we are acting at cross-purposes with our own intended self-interest."

—Richard Rohr,
A Spring Within Us: A Book of Daily Meditations

In an ancient fable from India a group of blind men came upon an elephant, which they had never encountered. Each began to explore this creature, eager to understand it. The first ran into the beast's broad and sturdy side. "It is clear," he said, "the elephant is like a massive wall." The second blind man grasped the elephant's sharp tusk. "The elephant is a great spear-like animal," he proclaimed. The third man had become entwined in its twisting trunk and yelled back, "no, it is clearly a snake!"

As he wrapped his arms around its massive leg another shook his head. "Really, the elephant is more like a tree." That one's friend was reeling from being swatted by the large flapping ear. "How can you not know the elephant is like a large fan?" Yet another blind man happened to catch the elephant's swinging tail. "You are all crazy. It is so plainly a rope-like animal." And on the

1

debate went, each holding to his view of the elephant, unwilling to understand the experience of another.

Never mind that an elephant so assaulted might have just crushed one or more of the blind men and run away. It is a fable. And it is meant to show us how our limited experiences shape the views we hold. Each of the blind men was partly correct. And they all were wrong.

Most of us live similarly blind lives when it comes to understanding what kind of creature we humans are. We define what we and others should be based on our own personality. All other ideas seem wrong or crazy. But our personality is limited. Unless we question it and try to experience things the way others do, we remain like those blind men.

The enneagram helps open our eyes

That is where the enneagram and this small book come in. The enneagram (pronounced n-ee-uh-gram) is an ancient and yet very modern system for understanding the personality. The word comes from Greek and means simply a model based on nine points. This system has been developed and refined over thousands of years and has recently become very popular in the U.S.

According to the enneagram, there are nine basic forms of personality. There are many variations on those nine forms. Within each of us, each of those energies exists to some degree— they are common human tendencies, so we all have them. But ultimately we each seem to be dominated by one of these patterns.

No one personality pattern is better or worse than the other. Each has its gifts and its traps. Just like each of the blind men experiences part of the truth of the elephant. The real challenge we face from these personality forms is our lack of awareness. Awareness that they dominate our way of seeing things. And awareness that others can have very different ways of seeing the world and very different patterns of thinking and acting that are just as real and right as ours.

The enneagram gives us a tool to begin to awaken to these personality-driven patterns.

Most of us begin this path wanting to know: "what type am I?" That's understandable and good. As you work through this guide, you will probably get a growing sense of which of these forms applies most to you. But if we stop there and become too focused on just which number represents us, we miss the point. For the enneagram to work its magic, we need an understanding of the whole elephant and not just a piece of it. I hope that as you learn about each different type you'll first see where its personality form shows up in your life. Maybe it is rare. Maybe it is a way of thinking or feeling that you dislike. But it is still likely to have some place in your life.

Then, as you deepen your appreciation for the ways each type understands and reacts to the world, you'll eventually see which one most fits your patterns. A number of enneagram teachers have described the moment of knowing your type as one of embarrassment, even humiliation. It certainly was for me. That feeling results from having your deepest drives and secret fears exposed—to yourself. When you do arrive at that understanding (and that can take a lot of exploration), my hope is that the path you walked to get there increases your understanding of others' challenges. If so, you will be able to use your knowledge more fruitfully for understanding yourself and others.

The enneagram is a path to forgiveness

In June 1959, a Tibetan Buddhist monk, Palden Gyatso, was arrested by Chinese officials for protesting their invasion of his homeland. He was imprisoned, and for the next 33 years he suffered horrific tortures from his captors. His body was broken and marred for life. In labor camps he was forced to work long hours with little food, even pulling an iron plow and being beaten like an animal. In 1992, he was released and then escaped to India. During an interview, this aged monk was asked what his greatest fear was during those painful years. His reply: that he would lose compassion for his torturers.

How does someone find that kind of forgiveness?

Forgiveness is not easy. It can be complicated. Many books have been written on how to forgive others and ourselves. This book will not answer all the questions about forgiveness. But perhaps it will add something helpful by looking at forgiving through a different lens.

The path to forgiveness begins with understanding

"Understanding?! If you only understood what was done to

me ... what I did ... you wouldn't talk about forgiveness. There is no way to accept it, to make sense of it, much less to forgive it! Maybe God can. But no person can, or should." Have you ever felt this way about the possibility of forgiveness?

The limited personality—some call it "ego"—is the ultimate con man. The stories of reality it tells us over and over are convincing. "Surely everyone else sees what we see. Right? How could it be otherwise? This is bad, that is good. I should be this way, you should be that way. It must be so for the world to make sense." When we are stuck in this only-one-way thinking, it is very difficult to understand or forgive anyone.

The enneagram shines a light on the games that our limited personality has played with us. Each of us has been and usually still is captive to a particular kind of game. These habitual games, or patterns of behavior, have served us in the past, helping us manage the world. But for most of us, there is a high cost to remaining stuck in our patterns.

By beginning to understand the workings of our ego and personality, and those of others, we can find a new freedom. This book is offered as a start on the lifelong process of getting free from the games of the limited personality. Free to discover the deeper authentic self inside you.

The enneagram is part of your spiritual journey

A word of warning: your ego-personality will go with you on this journey. At every twist in the path, it will try to make sure what you learn strengthens its hold on you. Too many people turn the enneagram into a game of finding their strengths and judging the weaknesses of other types. Or just the opposite: reinforcing their brokenness and the superiority of others. Either of these reactions keeps you from seeing the whole elephant.

To help break the hold of the blinded personality, this guide offers affirmations related to each type. I encourage you to try all the affirmations and exercises for the different types, both to feel others' worlds and to help you eventually find your particular type and free it.

The enneagram is much more than a personality typing system. It is meant to support you on your other personal paths of healing. Groups have used it as a complement to twelve-step programs by enhancing awareness of our addictive patterns, assisting our personal inventory, releasing our grievances and helping us to more wisely make amends.

The enneagram is also intended to be part of any spiritual journey. Each enneagram type has its unique ways to try to block our spiritual growth. True spiritual surrender asks us to live beyond the limits of one personality pattern. The enneagram offers a way to become aware of personality's forms and tricks so we can free ourselves to become our evolving authentic self.

May it bless your life and the lives of everyone around you.

The Enneagram's Nine Paths

"A path, unlike a road, does not move directly from point A to point B. Instead it adapts to the natural contours of the place in which it finds itself."

—Michael Jones, *The Soul of Place: Reimagining Leadership through Nature, Art and Community*

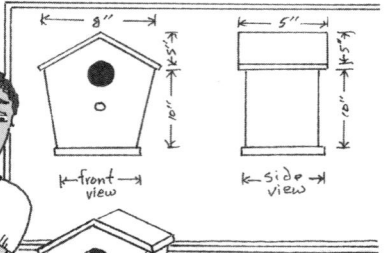

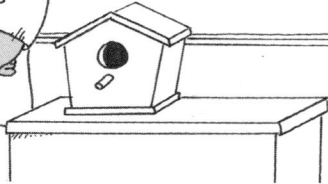

Type One: The Perfectionist

Gifts: Ones look to improve the world. They often see moral wrongs and are driven to make them right. They strive for honesty and goodness, in themselves first and then in others. Ones can lead others with an inspiring vision of what a better world can and should be.

Traps: The world is not perfect, and it never will be. Frustration — in themselves, in others, in the world — causes Ones to become impatient and judgmental. To others, Ones can seem controlling and simmering with anger, though the One is unlikely to admit to the anger. Anger is seen as a bad emotion. Instead, the One wants to be seen as a role model for doing things right. Ones find that over and over they have to "take up the slack" for people who don't live by their moral code. Resentment at living by the hard rules that others don't even see as necessary adds to the denied anger.

Most dreaded words: "You are a bad person."

Challenges for self-forgiveness: As with all types, Ones must first become aware of what is going on inside. The voices demanding perfection and goodness are powerful. At the first level, Ones must acknowledge and accept deep anger, resentment and judgment inside. Then Ones must see how at times they have lived directly opposite to their own moral code, all while preaching righteousness. It is hard work to release the idea that love is only earned through being good and right. Even when Ones realize the pain they have caused themselves with these internal rules, they will then have to deal with the ego-personality again. The inner personality voice will remind them of all the other people they have hurt with their controlling judgment, causing them to feel like a "bad" person again. Breaking that cycle is challenging.

Challenges for forgiving others: In order to avoid the horrible feeling of being wrong or bad themselves, Ones too often blame others. "If only they lived up to the standards, I wouldn't have gotten in this mess," the One's limited self whispers. Only through accepting that their "right" way of doing things is just "their" way of living can Ones release the trap of their controlling ways. By appreciating all the other enneagram types, their gifts and struggles, the One can begin to let go. In fact, with openness, Ones will find that they have often experienced the world the way others do. Only the limited personality has suppressed those feelings or made the One regret those moments of being free, or angry, or needy, or relaxed. The key to forgiveness of others for the One then is releasing the deeply held idea of perfection.

Affirmations for the One:

I let go of needing to be right.

I leg go of needing others to follow my rules.

I let go of judging others.

I let go of judging myself.

I let go of feeling like I'm not good enough.

I accept that I can be resentful and angry.

I accept that when we do our best, it is good enough.

I accept that I can learn from others.

I accept that being happy is more important than being right.

I accept that love is not earned but received.

I forgive myself for not being perfect.

I forgive others for doing the best they can.

Helpful Practices for Ones:

Ones hold much inside and try to always project a good version of themselves. This holding creates tension and numbness in the body. Any practice that connects the body to breath and feelings is helpful. Yoga or dance or other exercises that invite body awareness are great. Be willing to do it with minimal judgment and maximum joy. Ones who learn to be more playful and childlike reduce stress on themselves and those around them. Embracing the imperfections within and outside allows the One to lead others to a happier future for all.

Imagine a crowded TV room, with only one TV. Enneagram One is certain that he knows which show should be on—it's the best show and he could tell you many reasons why it's superior to the other programs.

Someone comes in and changes the channel without asking the group. One seethes with anger: that was a wrong thing to do and someone should teach that person how to act right!

Type Two: The Helper

Gifts: Twos love to take care of others. They are generous, committed to service, and can be very humble. A Two is a supportive friend in a time of need. Twos reflect back the best in other people and can inspire great achievements.

Traps: Underneath the giving nature of Twos lurks an insecure ego that needs to be needed. Being needed is how Twos believe they find love. So jealousy is a trap for some Twos. Their insecurity can cause the Two to manipulate others, especially with flattery. Getting too involved with other people's emotional lives is another sign of this challenge. The Two can also become addicted to praise. The humble aspect of the Two hides a pride that can be mean when it doesn't get what it wants. Deep down, Twos have needs that are denied so they can just be there for others. Martyrdom and anger pop up when the Two's personal needs are ignored for too long.

Most dreaded words: "You aren't needed or loved."

Challenges for self-forgiveness: Because so much of the Two's image depends on being seen as unselfish, generous and thoughtful, admitting to the darker motives of the personality can be very difficult. In the Two's universe, thinking about one's own needs and admitting to pride ends the chance of being loved. That is scary. So Twos must learn that they are loved and lovable no matter what. Not admitting to these other needs and motives actually makes those drives stronger as they control things from within the personality's shadows. With work, a Two can find self-worth and love that better supports helping others without being dependent on how others respond.

Challenges for forgiving others: People who either refuse the help of the Two or aren't thankful enough can trigger hurt and anger in the Two. Understanding that it is not the duty of others to make the Two feel worthy or loved is crucial to forgiving others. Twos are caught in a deeper bind, as well. On the one hand they seek to be close to people whose problems they can help solve. The appreciation they get feeds them. On the other hand they try not to be needy themselves and deep down feel superior to those who do need them. Forgiving others for being human and needing support and help requires Twos to also admit their own needs and stop shaming themselves for having needs.

Affirmations for the Two:

I let go of expecting others to affirm my worth.

I let go of manipulating people to be needed.

I let go of being jealous and controlling.

I let go of denying my motives, emotions and needs.

I let go of making others feel guilty for not appreciating me enough.

I accept that I am loved and lovable just as I am.

I accept that caring for myself is not selfish but healing.

I accept that I can love and care for others without expecting anything back.

I accept that others will be there to help me when I need it, if I ask clearly.

I accept that I naturally have much love and joy to share.

I forgive myself for having needs and depending on others for help.

I forgive others for not responding to my help in the ways I wish.

Helpful Practices for Twos:

Twos have trouble admitting to their motives, emotions and needs. Journaling can help reveal what is going on inside. Setting a time period each day — even just ten minutes — to write out what has happened and how you feel about it is a good practice. Focus on why you did or said things. Dare to confess your real needs and wants. This might be done after a short, quiet meditation. Become aware enough to pause before responding to someone's request for help. Ask whether you truly want to offer or are doing it to feel needed or praised. This practice will help bring a Two back into balance. A Two who embraces the balance of giving and receiving becomes a true helper to everyone.

Imagine that crowded TV room again. Two is feeling happy because he's here with his friend Joe. Joe likes the Lakers, and suddenly Two feels interested in watching the basketball game. "This is fun! I like the Lakers too!" Two doesn't stop to think about whether he's ever been interested in basketball before. He enjoys asking Joe about the game and congratulating him on how much he knows and what great taste he has in basketball teams.

Someone comes in and changes the channel. Two is sympathetic with the channel changer and the people who get mad at him. He wishes he could help all of them feel better.

20

Type Three: The Achiever

Gifts: Threes strive to succeed. They are talented, confident, attract others to them, and rally everyone to win. A motivated Three will figure out the best way to achieve something, organize tasks to get there, and work hard to see it through. People admire the positive spirit Threes bring to everything. A three is very good at figuring out what a group of people needs from them and then willingly taking on those roles.

Traps: Success is not possible in everything. In fact, the greatest successes come after many failures. That reality is not acceptable to most Threes. Too often the appearance of success is more important than the truth of it. So when difficulties arise, Threes can abandon the work if it risks exposing faults and failures. Or they will lie to themselves and others about how it is all going, keeping a good face on things. At a deeper level, a Three uses all the trappings of success to hide a fear of being unworthy. What if there really is nothing of value and substance below the surface? The fear of being found out and exposed as a fake is powerful.

Most dreaded words: "You are worthless."

Challenges for self-forgiveness: No one can be successful and admired all the time. Yet that is exactly what the Three expects. Any crack in the smiling face the Three presents to the world is unacceptable. So Threes typically stay far away from their real feelings. Once the world makes them experience failure and loss of control, as it always will, Threes feel devastated. A gang of humiliating voices inside can rise threatening to expose how unworthy they are. Only by giving up the constant pursuit of praise and admitting to their limitations can Threes begin to understand their true nature. Eventually they can forgive themselves for making mistakes and not being the best at everything. Threes are worthy and lovable just as they are. Of course, then they can also see and really value the special gifts they do have to share with others.

Challenges for forgiving others: As with some other enneagram types, Threes depend on the reactions of others to keep their self-esteem high. When others fail to respond the way they need, Threes will feel betrayed, even if smiling the whole time. Threes, while unaware of their own feelings, are very aware of others' feelings. Some people simply don't care about success at all costs like the Three. Others sense the shallow ways Threes act or commit to friendships and feel used by Threes. Finally, there are those who will get more credit and praise, even if not competing directly with the Three. All those people are threats to the Three's public face. So Threes may target these obstacles to their image of success and undercut them. Once all of these ego games come into awareness, the Three can begin to forgive others for not wanting to play by the same impossible rules. With time, Threes can also see that people are willing to value them for being real, with faults and limitations. In fact, that honesty is the only way they can fully trust the relationship with the Three. Instead of a threat, others' ability to see and accept the "messy" version of the Three becomes a gift.

Affirmations for the Three:

I let go of needing to appear successful at all costs.

I let go of seeing others as threats.

I let go of hiding my failures and limitations.

I let go of having to be admired and denying my real feelings.

I let go of fearing I'm unworthy and unlovable.

I accept that my value is much more than my image.

I accept that real success includes failures.

I accept that others will love me when I'm honest and open.

I accept that I am worthy just the way I am.

I accept that I share my gifts for the good of everyone.

I forgive myself for having feelings, faults and limitations.

I forgive others for not making me feel good about myself all the time.

Helpful Practices for Threes:

As doers, always striving for the next goal, Threes need to learn to disconnect. Meditation, especially the kind that has no goal but just sitting and observing feelings, is great medicine. But, of course, it will not be easy for the average Three. Creative work, like art, where there is no audience to impress but just done for private satisfaction, will also help. Join in group activities where you are not the leader and instead do routine work to help with the good of all. Volunteer activities like this can help you see how your more "common" capabilities are valuable and how others' approaches also contribute in ways you may not have valued before. Freed from image and ego, a Three can accomplish greater things than ever imagined.

In the crowded TV room, Three notices that an interest in and knowledge of basketball is admired by this group. Three begins talking about the games he's been to in the past, hinting that he's been invited to sit near the team at a Lakers game or hang out with them after the game. He doesn't notice that his real interest is somewhere else today. He gets energized by showing the group what an expert he is in basketball strategy. Three begins to figure out how to start a basketball league on the unit.

Unless there's a way to shine as the person who solved the problem, Three isn't very interested in a conflict over changed channels.

Type Four: The Individualist

Gifts: The Four is often creative, an artist, with a keen eye for beauty. Unlike many other types they are highly sensitive to emotions, both their own and others'. Life is meant for deep, authentic connections, Fours believe. They can be romantics, giving rich patterns of meaning to what others see as ordinary. A Four stands out as an original, with a special style and view of things.

Traps: It is a thin line between the romantic and the tragic. Fours waver on that line. On the one hand, a Four can be an intense partner in a relationship, paying attention to every detail and caring about every feeling. On the other hand, that deep connection feels betrayed when others fail to value the relationship in the same way the Four does. It can feel that the delicate beauty of the world is ruined by others who are insensitive and brutal. Fours can also become obsessed with their own shortcomings, growing to hate themselves for flaws and defects. When relationships fall apart, Fours can believe their flaws were the cause for rejection. This internal struggle leads some Fours to be wary of connecting with others at all.

Most dreaded words: "You're nothing special."

Challenges for self-forgiveness: Fours love to tell stories. Especially to themselves. Over and over. Unfortunately, most of those stories are about how deeply ruined and pointless things are when they could be so beautiful and meaningful. And most of those stories are about themselves. Fours can obsess on one comment that seemed critical or insensitive and build it into deep self-hatred. For Fours to overcome the feeling of not being that special person they dream of, they must first understand that they are unique just as they are. Of course, everyone else is, too. That's where the Four personality gets really upset. But the Four still has special talents and unique perspectives to share. The Four must also learn to observe feelings without adding energy to them. Without turning them into a story and inflating them, emotions come and pass by, like the weather.

Challenges for forgiving others: The world fails Fours. People fail Fours, again and again. It is hard for Fours to understand why others aren't as aware of the pain or the potential of life as they are. Forgiving others for being themselves requires the Four to truly embrace the specialness of everyone. We all have different goals and ways of trying to fulfill them. The Four must also stop looking down on those who don't live as deeply or emotionally as the Four does. In fact, Fours can learn better emotional balance from others. To be in successful relationships, Fours must forgive others for flaws and fears while also doing the same for themselves. They must also learn to accept, even value, the "normal" or "ordinary" people and events in life. Finally Fours need to admit to and release envy when constantly comparing to others.

Affirmations for the Four:

I let go of needing to be special.

I let go of hating myself for being flawed.

I let go of telling myself negative stories over and over.

I let go of feeling superior for being more sensitive than
others.

I let go of retreating into fantasies and depression.

I accept that I am unique even with my defects.

I accept that my emotions don't rule my life.

I accept that there is beauty and meaning in everything and
everybody.

I accept that I have much to offer the world, just as I am.

I accept that others have much to teach me about different
ways to experience life.

I forgive myself for envying others and shaming myself.

I forgive others for not understanding all my deepest pains
and hopes.

Helpful Practices for Fours:

One of the most important things for Fours to do is to
become less involved with their emotions. A meditation that can
help involves bringing up a single strong emotion, not difficult for
most Fours. A story of wrongs likely will come with it. Indulge
that story. Let it build. Then stop. That will be the hard part.
Refuse to give any more energy to the emotion. Ignore it. How
long does it last without that extra energy? Where do you feel it
in your body, and what does it feel like when it fades? Fours can
also stop self-sabotage by setting realistic goals on projects and

completing them, even it if feels less "amazing" than dreamed of. Reaching out and volunteering to help others in need can help Fours see that everyone has ups and downs and yet most still push on. A Four grounded in realistic expectations and present emotions gives gifts to others that are unique and meaningful.

In the crowded TV room, Four is feeling dramatic and upset. Why don't these people notice that I have a story to tell that's more beautiful and interesting than a basketball game? If only they understood my unique situation. I could have them all in tears if they'd listen to this poem I wrote earlier today. We could connect so deeply if we shared our feelings. This noisy game is hurting my ears and hurting my feelings.

Conflict starts on the other side of the room, over someone changing a channel. Four folds into himself, wondering why bad things always happen to him and why these guys want to ruin his day.

32

Type Five: The Investigator

Gifts: Fives have a passion for knowledge and ideas. When they focus their keen intellects, they gather data needed to understand and solve problems. Fives also create new ways of seeing things that can inspire better ways to work and live. They have an objective approach that makes them good listeners.

Traps: The world isn't a computer responding to the right data. It is filled with messy emotions and decisions that aren't based on logic. The typical Five is unnerved by such a world. Fives are wary of being too close to people who are unpredictable and emotional. Such people unsettle things too much. Fives instead withdraw into their quiet place and gather more and more information as a defense. The Five is intent on figuring a way out of the chaos. Even emotional problems, when the Five can see them, must be solved with knowledge. When knowing isn't enough, the Five can become hopeless and isolated.

Most dreaded words: "You don't know anything useful."

Challenges for self-forgiveness: Fives are driven by a deep insecurity about being smart enough or good enough at things. The emotions of fear and anxiety that come with that insecurity are too much to bear, so the Five shuts them down and seeks to be objective. The first challenge for the Five is accepting that these emotions are real and okay to feel. Everyone has insecurities. The Five must let go of having to master something at a level that can't be doubted. No matter how much we know about something, there is probably much more no one understands. Fives must embrace uncertainty, even mystery. Saying "I don't know" and not judging oneself for it is a big step toward self-forgiveness.

Challenges for forgiving others: Fives pretend not to care what others think, but deep down they really do. That others don't recognized their genius and mastery really hurts. Or when they do admire the Five's abilities, there is always the risk they will intrude too much into the Five's world and mess it up. So the Five generally keeps people at arm's length. That distance makes it too easy to judge and dismiss people. Instead, the Five must risk connection. Fives must aim the desire to understand things toward others, realizing all that others have to teach Fives. Fives must try to see them not as objects of study but as fellow humans, struggling to figure out their own problems. Doing so with openness can lead Fives to not only accept others closer into their world, but also to accept themselves as emotional beings.

Affirmations for the Five:

I let go of needing to know everything.

I let go of distancing myself from others.

I let go of fearing emotions.

I let go of living inside my head.

I let go of arguing with others so they will admit I'm right.

I accept that it is okay to say 'I don't know'.

I accept that the world is full of uncertainty and mystery.

I accept that I am useful and lovable.

I accept that others can teach me.

I accept that I have as much to offer from my heart as from my head.

I forgive myself for hiding my best self from the world.

I forgive others for expressing their emotions.

Helpful Practices for Fives:

The ability to be at peace, especially when the world around them is not, is important for Fives. One practice might be to practice meditation in noisy places. In a room filled with others, you might sit in the corner with eyes closed and for just a few minutes breath calmly while noticing every noise, every word, every gust of air as someone walks by, every smell, and don't categorize or judge them. Just notice. With eyes open, you might write down all the different kinds of clothing or colors on the walls. Being present to reality and not escaping into thoughts help Fives participate in the world. Also, Fives need to get into their bodies, so physical exercise of all kinds can help. Finally, Fives can "study" emotions, but only if they feel them and understand them inside. Then, and only then, can knowledge become wisdom. A Five equipped with this deeper understanding can solve the most difficult problems of the world.

Five doesn't stay long in the crowded TV room unless there's a show on about science or history or how things work. He'd much rather be reading an informative book than watching a basketball game.

Someone comes in and changes the channel. Five is curious, watching how this is going to unfold so he can understand the ways of this unit.

Type Six: The Loyalist

Gifts: Sixes can be trusted to support a group and remain loyal to principles. They think through possible challenges and prepare different ways of meeting them. They will fight for a cause they believe in and defend their family and community. Sixes make loyal friends.

Traps: The world is an unpredictable, dangerous place to a Six. By aligning with a group, a belief, religion, or a leader, Sixes find security and support. But they also worry about how strong or long-lasting that support will be, so they can suddenly question and doubt the group. There is a deep conflict in Sixes between giving themselves over to others and yet not trusting others and rebelling. They may turn against the leader or group if they feel things are changing too much or people aren't living up to the implied ideals. Individual relations can fall prey to the same tensions. Sixes may sabotage relationships just to end the tension of not being sure where they stand. They may also foolishly run into danger to try to overcome their deep fear of it.

Most dreaded words: "We no longer need you or want you."

Challenges for self-forgiveness: At the core, Sixes doubt their ability to make it on their own. A Six works hard to become worthy of being part of the group. But at the same time, the Six dreads how quickly it could all be taken away. That doubt can lead to self-defeating actions. Which only make the insecurity worse. To stop the cycle, Sixes must face their fears. Not in the rash way, but in a rational way. Yes, the world is unpredictable and sometimes dangerous, but it is also supportive and loving. Everyone else lives in the same world and many do so without the same anxiety. How? They have confidence. In themselves and in the world. There are never guarantees that all will work out as hoped. But all can be worked through. Sixes must own that they are stronger than they think. They have the internal resources to deal with challenges on their own. They often have the best advice to give themselves, if they will just learn to listen and trust it.

Challenges for forgiving others: Sixes are dependent on others to give them security and meaning. Because of that, they are very prone to feeling abandoned and betrayed. Giving others so much power over their well-being, Sixes can become fierce foes if they think they've been crossed. Yet, people's words and actions are often at odds. Sixes must see how fickle they can be too. And the Six needs to stop turning over power to others who are, after all, human, too. Other people can be helpful and supportive. Belief systems can provide guidance. But that help and guidance cannot make the decisions Sixes must make for themselves. Sixes need to stop blaming others for problems and trust in their own ability to deal with challenges.

Affirmations for the Six:

I let go of depending on others to feel safe.

I let go of doubting my inner strength.

I let go of overreacting to problems, both real and imagined.

I let go of blaming others for my fears and problems.

I let go of looking for betrayals and turning against people.

I accept that I can face the uncertain with self-confidence.

I accept that I can make my own decisions.

I accept that others can help me but don't define me.

I accept that I help others out of goodwill, not need.

I accept that what doesn't work out can be worked through.

I forgive myself for living in fear when I have so much inner strength.

I forgive others for not making the world secure for me.

Helpful Practices for Sixes:

The first challenge of Sixes is dealing with almost constant anxiety. Meditation, seated or walking in nature, as a regular practice will help ground that energy. Stop trying to create and solve problems in your head. Just experience the moment. Try new things, like sports or games or art, anything that you might be afraid of at first. With time, Sixes can gain self-confidence at facing the new and uncertain. Journal about how it feels to face and then overcome these new activities. Be sure to give yourself credit for sticking to it (especially when things don't go as you want). In group settings, make a point of saying something positive about a situation before talking about all the things that are or might go wrong. A Six facing these challenges will be appreciated even more for the dependable gifts shared with others.

In the TV room, Six is enjoying watching the game. He likes being in the group, but worries that something could go wrong. A few years ago somebody changed the channel and a fight started. What if that happens now? What if I get blamed for it or hurt in the fight? I'll keep enjoying watching with the group, but I'll keep an eye out for trouble, Six thinks to himself.

The things Six feared start to happen, and a fight is breaking out. Six is surprisingly calm. He's been expecting something like this.

Type Seven: The Enthusiast

Gifts: Sevens are joyful and spontaneous, always open to a new adventure. They want to experience and share the best the world has to offer. They spread optimism. Sevens like to list and plan, move quickly from task to task and get a lot done, especially if they aren't required to get bogged down on one piece of work.

Traps: Though they say they savor life, most Sevens don't stay with any one thing long enough to truly appreciate it deeply. That is because they are afraid of the pain and despair that might await them in stillness. While all types can be addicts, the Seven is especially prone to becoming addicted to things that momentarily make them feel better. Even if not to a substance, Sevens can be generally addicted to constant stimulation. They are greedy for experiences, friends, food, wins, and/or things. A Seven doesn't want to miss any opportunity to feel good or to check off something on the list and move on. They don't usually stop distracting themselves until they run out of money, friends, or health. Life will never be all highs, and Sevens find this truth very distressing.

Most dreaded words: "You need to stop and feel how much this hurts."

Challenges for self-forgiveness: At some point, most Sevens exhaust themselves. They can't distract themselves any longer. What is left is all the darkness and pain that has been denied and neglected. It feels like torture to a Seven. The last thing a Seven wants is to wallow in feelings and sorrows. But those deeper voices must be heard for healing. The built up pain can feel over-whelming. Accepting all the parts of themselves that have been neglected and abused in favor of momentary highs is hard for Sevens. Sevens in this place can become very judgmental toward themselves, even self-hating. They may then go looking for ways to blame it all on others. Yet with patience and growing faith that the world is much richer and joy is much deeper when connected to inevitable pain and disappointment, the Seven can find self-forgiveness.

Challenges for forgiving others: In the normal flow of their lives, Sevens get frustrated with others who seem to block their fun. They may lash out at those people, like a child being told to eat a carrot instead of a cookie. And while they see themselves as the life of the party, others, especially those trying to be close to them, may see them as shallow and disloyal. Sevens are notorious for having backup plans, ready to ditch one friend if another person with a better option comes along. Anyone trying to talk through their feelings will seem whiney or a bore to the Seven. So once these patterns are seen by Sevens, it can be really painful to admit to the pain they have caused others. All the Seven ever wanted was to bring joy into the world and avoid pain. How could that hurt anyone? Owning that it has hurt others will be difficult. But it is crucial to forgiving others for experiencing life differently and wanting deeper connections.

Affirmations for the Seven:

I let go of my need for constant distractions.

I let go of my destructive addictions.

I let go of dismissing others as boring or whiney.

I let go of fearing I won't have enough.

I let go of avoiding feelings.

I accept that life is full of both ups and downs.

I accept that joy is deeper when pain is allowed in too.

I accept that choosing one thing doesn't deprive me of another.

I accept that others have rich lives that I can be inspired by.

I accept that I am loved even when I'm not the life of the party.

I forgive myself for hurting myself and others in order to avoid difficult feelings.

I forgive others for showing me the darker sides of the world and myself.

Helpful Practices for Sevens:

The most helpful practice for Sevens is their most dreaded: being in stillness and feeling. So this should be done a little at a time. Just committing to a three- or five-minute meditation once a day can begin to work wonders for a Seven. The fears of what awaits the undistracted mind begin to calm. It may be dark in there, but it is not unmanageable. To build confidence that life can be lived without constant short-lived highs, the Seven can practice appreciating simple things. A single flower, if looked at closely, can provide as much magic as a whole bouquet. Or what about an unusual picture in a magazine or a piece of music? The Seven can learn to savor more deeply, especially when not afraid of feelings that might come along with that deeper experience. Also finding at least a few friends where there is a commitment to deeper connections can be important. Learn to have longer talks that include sharing both joys and sorrows so that both feel accepted for the full range of emotions. Avoid trying to cheer up the other person or solve the problems. In the end, Sevens can realize they have a much deeper joy to share than they ever thought possible.

Seven is super excited to watch this game! His favorite team is playing and he's sure they're going to win. He is right up front, laughing with the other guys and cheering every basket his team makes.

Someone comes in and changes the channel. Seven doesn't see that—he got bored when his team got behind by 10 points, and he's down the hall playing cards.

Type Eight: The Challenger

Gifts: Eights are strong, dominating, self-willed, and big-hearted. They often champion the underdog, defending those others disregard or abuse. Eights can make unrelenting competitors and commanding leaders.

Traps: The world chews up and spits out the weak. That is what an Eight believes. To an Eight, there is nothing worse than being helpless. So Eights become fierce and powerful to fight off whatever comes at them. That stance may be necessary in extreme situations. Treating all of life that way, as Eights do, is sure to backfire. Eights attack both foes and friends. They look for wrongs to right, creating conflict where it wasn't. An Eight sees this as noble and courageous. Others see it as controlling and hostile. Eights eventually lose allies and friends. In the end, Eights face the world alone, more vulnerable for having alienated others. In response to that rejection, Eights hardens their hearts even more. And so the cycle continues.

Most dreaded words: "You are weak, ineffective and not in control."

Challenges for self-forgiveness: Apologizing is a sign of weakness to Eights. So getting to a place of even considering self-forgiveness takes lots of work. "What is there to forgive?", asks the Eight. "I've only protected myself and those I care about from a threatening world." Along the way, though, the Eight has likely also unnecessarily hurt others. Often those closest get the worst of it. And Eights wear themselves out with the constant need to battle and control. It is exhausting. There is a very tender heart inside every Eight longing to be protected in a more gentle way. Eights must access that tenderness and stop being afraid of it. They must learn about strength that is quieter and more confident. Reacting with anger and fighting are really driven more by fear than strength. True strength stays steady under pressure knowing just how much force is needed to keep things in good balance.

Challenges for forgiving others: To the average Eight, other people are to be challenged, protected, or led. Those who are challenged must be bested. Those who are protected must never turn into challengers. And those in between should follow the Eight or get out of the way. As much as any of the personality types, Eights must come to value and appreciate all the other types and their particular strengths. The Eight has to break the "my way or the highway" mentality to see how powerful all gifts are in their own ways. All the energies of the enneagram types are within the Eight, too. By forgiving others for not being what Eights define as strong, Eights actually free their own hidden strengths. Eights will then be able to get their deepest needs met. True intimacy requires openness. Openness requires quiet confidence. Quiet confidence requires deep, true strength.

Affirmations for the Eight:

I let go of controlling and abusing others.

I let go of reacting with anger and rage.

I let go of believing that having feelings makes you weak.

I let go of seeing the world as unsafe.

I let go of needing to prevail at all costs.

I accept that my heart is as big and strong as my will.

I accept that I long for closeness with others.

I accept that deep down I am often afraid.

I accept that other people's strength is not always a threat to me.

I accept that helping people requires letting them have their own power.

I forgive myself for reacting so strongly to my own fear of being controlled and dismissed.

I forgive others for expressing their strengths in ways different from mine.

Helpful Practices for Eights:

Eights are driven by intensity. Whether in work, play or relationships, they give it their all. But it can be overwhelming to others and exhausting for the Eight. Like Sevens, Eights need to slow down and feel their inner life. Meditation, walks outside, or any activity that is for enjoyment, not competition, is helpful. In personal relations, Eights need to first become aware of just how loving and caring their heart really is. That comes from looking inward, honestly and fearlessly. Then they have to develop the courage to risk sharing that heart with someone else. The real test will be when the reactions aren't exactly what the Eight wanted. Then they will have to find the inner confidence to stay open anyway. It takes time to develop mutual trust. But for the Eight, the reward is a world that is much less threatening and a heart that is much more at peace. Then the Eight becomes a true leader, building confidence and strength in others.

The TV room is crowded, but Eight isn't there yet.

Eight walks in and changes the channel. He didn't consult with anyone first—he's used to taking charge. If anyone challenges his right to take charge, he's ready for a fight. He craves intensity and he'd rather be in a fight than be bored.

Type Nine: The Peacemaker

Gifts: Nines bring harmony to the world. They value others' different ways of thinking and like to balance their various views. Nines are patient, supportive, humble and help others to be their best.

Traps: In the effort to bring peace and harmony, Nines avoid conflicts. They don't assert themselves and defer to others. Often they lose any true sense of what they think, feel, and would fight for. When the world throws conflict at them, Nines try to escape. They withdraw into inner fantasies. They can give up on work or relationships if they are too much trouble. Or they can just go along with the most forceful people around them, hiding their resistance and resentment. A Nine cornered by anger will try to make everything okay while looking for a way out. Nines can also just go numb, blocking all feeling. Distracting activities or drugs can be used to medicate against the discomforts of feeling.

Most dreaded words: "You are self-centered and make me angry."

Challenges for self-forgiveness: Because Nines ignore their own feelings, it can be difficult to be aware of their own range of emotions and motives in life. Behind the peaceful front are often resentment, anger, competitiveness, hurt, judgment — really all the feelings of other types. But Nines are the last to admit to these. By avoiding the darkness and conflict in the world, they've avoided seeing it in themselves. It will take some time to find the safety to look at these deeper feelings. When they tap into these energies, Nines realize all the ways they've undercut themselves. They have to own how many times they haven't stood up for a belief, taken credit for their good work, or confronted a bully. Nines also have to own how stubborn they have been with others in refusing to engage. That frustrates others, who are often seen by Nines for being reactive and angry. Yet Nines must see how they have helped trigger those reactions by refusing to be emotionally present and direct. Even the most locked down Nines can eventually explode with emotions, surprising even themselves. Forgiving those outbursts will require embracing how normal it is for most people to live through a range of emotions.

Challenges for forgiving others: Most Nines will say they already forgive others for the way they are. They don't want to dwell on wrongs too much. It is just too messy to dredge old things up. And there is no point to it. They may even have a spiritual philosophy they follow that tells them to let it all go. And on the surface that is probably just what they do. But at a deeper level that claim is too often not true. To know that there is anything to forgive others for, the Nine will have to admit being hurt and wronged. And with those feelings will come others, like anger and rage. All that is the opposite of peace and harmony, so the typical Nine will stop right there and dismiss needing to forgive anyone for anything. Yet if Nines can push on and awaken to their own feelings, Nines will find true forgiveness of others. That kind of forgiveness will actually release old emotions, not just paper over them. Others will notice this more authentic energy.

That can lead to more real power. A Nine who has done this work can stand up to those who are truly threatening. And that Nine can be more deeply connected to those who are supportive. The Nine may even discover that some of those who seem threatening are actually asking for a real response and a closer relationship.

Affirmations for the Nine:

I let go of needing everything to be calm and peaceful.

I let go of avoiding conflict.

I let go of hiding myself so others feel comfortable.

I let go of numbing out and giving up.

I let go of going along with others and not knowing what I want.

I accept that I have all the same emotions as others.

I accept that I can keep myself safe within conflict.

I accept that I will be more at peace by facing difficult emotions.

I accept that I am independent and capable of doing great things.

I accept that I bring people together best by being unafraid and my real self.

I forgive myself for avoiding my emotions and not asserting my own needs and goals.

I forgive others for creating conflicts that I can't always make right.

Helpful Practices for Nines:

Unlike for many others, meditation may seem to come easily to Nines. Yet it often takes the form of "blissing out" or escaping the real conflicts and emotions of life. Not really helpful for Nines. So a Nine must undertake work that is body-centered. Yoga can help connect the Nine to where in the body emotions have been stored and ignored for so long. It is important to hold poses long enough to feel some discomfort at the edge and breathe through the emotions that come up. A more traditional seated meditation can then focus on those areas in the body where emotions have been discovered. Stay alert to what is coming up. Don't go to sleep or zone out. Follow a repeated process of discovering then feeling emotions through the body. This process will help Nines become less and less afraid of conflict and emotions, both inside themselves and in others. Over time this will also allow Nines to be aware of what they really want or believe and have the courage to assert it to others. A Nine unafraid of emotions and conflict is truly empowered to bring peace to the world.

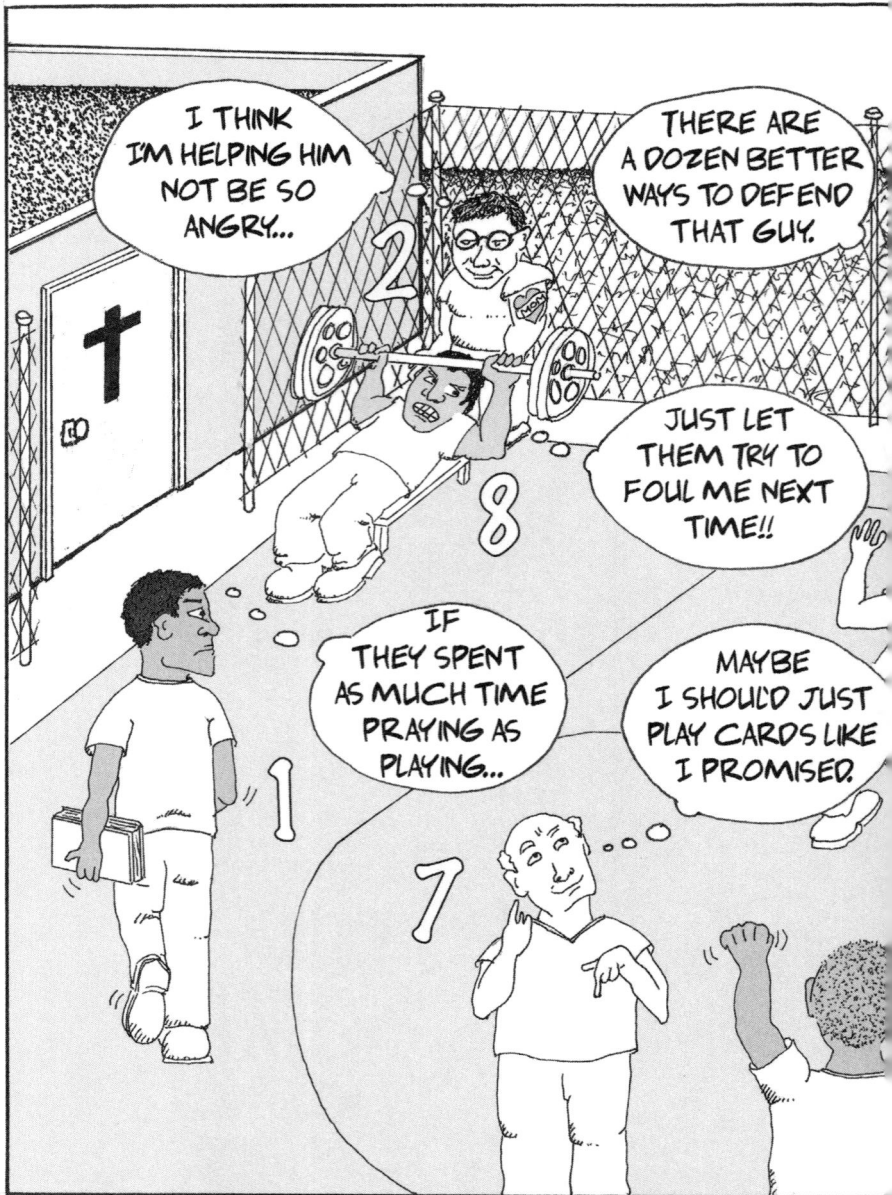

I'M UNSTOPPABLE!!
WHY CAN'T I BE NORMAL LIKE ALL OF THEM?
I CAN'T BELIEVE HE PICKED ME FOR HIS TEAM!
I SHOULD LEAVE SO IT 'LL BE AN EVEN NUMBER FOR THE NEXT GAME.
4
5
3
6
9

Rewriting Our Stories

"The enneagram does not put us in a box, it shows us the box we are already in—and the way out."

Riso/Hudson, The Wisdom of the Enneagram

We live our lives in stories. Whether you are sitting on your sofa at home or sitting on your bunk in prison, you are likely caught up in stories you tell yourself and others. Who am I? How did I get here? Why did I do what I did to others? Why did others do what they did to me?

All these questions ask us to make up a story, to make sense of a string of events and decisions that ended up with us siting here in this place at this time. So how true are the stories you've made up to answer those questions? Even if the pure facts of events are accurate, how confident are you of your motives or the motives of others?

If you've read closely so far in this brief description of the enneagram, you've probably begun to question some of the stories you've constructed. At least I hope so.

Even if you aren't yet confident about which type most fits you, being aware that there are vastly different ways of seeing the world may cause you to pause. Most of us act and react, unaware of the core fears, passions, and hopes that drive us. The enneagram is a powerful tool for making us aware of these drivers. With that awareness comes the ability to see through the stories we have become so attached to.

I can't count the number of times I have questioned my stories over the last twenty years. That's about how long I've known about the enneagram's way of understanding people. I've re-imagined some of my stories multiple times. I realize that my motives weren't always as pure as I wanted to believe. And I've also had to reconsider the motives I've put on others. When I realized their probable type and the deep fears that may have driven them, I've had to change my tune. So many actions that I took personally weren't really about me. And so much that I did for "good reasons" turned out to be about feeding my own personality's image. (I'm a One, by the way, so being good and right are often too important to me). This process is ongoing. It helps my relationships with family, friends, work colleagues, with people I don't agree with politically, and even with the Divine. In the end, it gives me greater compassion for others and for myself.

The path to understanding how our personality type affects us is long and winding. What is presented in this book provides a beginning.

Thousands upon thousands of pages have been written about all the powerful layers of understanding possible through the enneagram. Reading other books can be helpful. It has been for me. But the most important work is not reading. It is feeling. No matter what type each of us is, recognizing deeply what fears, desires and hopes are at our own core is key. Making the effort to see the world through others' eyes awakens further insights. Both acts, if practiced over and over, become transforming. And they are the gateways to true forgiveness.

Working with the enneagram calms our fears, opens our compassion, enriches our stories, and, through grace, helps us to live a deeper spiritual life as well.

How Human Kindness Foundation Uses the Enneagram

— by Catherine Dumas,
Executive Director, Human Kindness Foundation

In 2010 I was somewhat familiar with the enneagram, but hadn't paid a lot of attention. There are always ideas to explore and books to read—more than I can possibly keep up with. Then our friend and long-time Human Kindness Foundation volunteer Ann H. brought some recordings to the office, highly recommending them. Since I know how wise and insightful Ann is, I decided to give it a try.

I listened to those recordings one afternoon at home while recovering from an illness. They were talks by Father Richard Rohr, a wonderful teacher on many spiritual subjects including the enneagram. Some of the energies he described fit us so perfectly! I couldn't wait to talk to Sita about it, so I called: "You need to hear this with me!" Sita drove to my house right then, we listened together, and we both knew this was going to be important to us.

Sita and I have been friends since the mid-1980s. We've worked together closely and even for a while lived together. We are family, though not the kind that's born together, and we love each other. Like most family members, we don't always agree. We sometimes had a hard time even understanding each other, almost as if we spoke different languages.

It was frustrating and humbling. Here we were, two people of goodwill who genuinely like each other, who are committed to spiritual practices, who work together toward the goals of Human Kindness Foundation. With all that going for us, there were times when we simply could not understand each other. We hit the same roadblocks over and over even though we talked them through at length and tried to compromise.

Father Rohr's recording opened our eyes to a big point we were missing. Sita and I are different enneagram types, and no matter how closely aligned our values are, we're still looking at situations out of very different eyes. The exact same external situation looks like one sort of problem to her and a very different sort of problem to me. No wonder we had so much trouble finding solutions that worked for both of us!

As we spent time studying and reflecting on the enneagram, we learned ways to talk about our differences. We could finally understand why certain mundane issues were ongoing, unsolvable problems for us. We couldn't see the same problem, so how could we find a common solution?

We didn't stop seeing things from the perspective of our primary numbers, so we still work to understand each other's viewpoint. The enneagram is a tremendously helpful tool as we do that work. To use Chris's example of the elephant: we spend a lot less time in the Human Kindness Foundation office arguing about whether we've got a trunk or a tail. We know it's an elephant that each of us is touching from a different place. We still might not know what to do about the elephant, but we can honor and understand each viewpoint. We can forgive the other for not seeing it our way. Maybe, with our ongoing practices, we can forgive ourselves for not seeing the whole picture.

Since that afternoon in 2010 we have wanted to share this helpful tool with our friends. We are grateful to Chris Canfield for sharing his time and talent to make this book a reality. We're also thankful to Tom Dodson, Doug Meffert, and many friends who helped us explore the enneagram over these years.

A tool for forgiveness, Chris's title, is also my hope for this book. Use it as a tool, friends. When someone on your unit does something annoying—WHY does he make so much noise so early in the morning? WHY does she use the phone so long when I'm waiting for it?—instead of getting angry, get curious. Look back at this book and see if you can understand what enneagram energy that action came from. Does that make it easier to forgive? What about your own unskillful actions? Which enneagram energy did that particular action arise from (it may not be your primary number)? Can you understand your motivation in that moment in a way that helps you forgive yourself?

Whatever enneagram type you are, we love you and we hope this book is helpful in your spiritual journey.

A Word About Finding Your Number

Many people are tempted to use the enneagram like a puzzle-game: find their number and maybe the numbers of a few friends, then consider it "solved." We encourage you to use this tool in a more patient and ongoing way.

Each of the nine numbers is a human characteristic, and all of us humans share some of that trait. You will have more of some energies and less of others, and if you stick with it you are likely to discover that you have a primary number. Don't rush yourself! It can be helpful to look at how each of the energies expresses in your behavior.

The staff of Human Kindness Foundation wants this book to be your tool for better understanding—and forgiving— yourself and the people around you.

About the Author

Chris Canfield was introduced to the enneagram by Father Richard Rohr in the 1990s. Soon after, he began volunteering in prisons, leading yoga and meditation groups. He discovered the works of Bo Lozoff and eventually became a board member of the Human Kindness Foundation. Chris has read numerous books, attended multiple workshops, and facilitated discussions about the enneagram with his wife, Kate Finlayson, who created the Dancing the Enneagram playshop. Kate has studied with the Enneagram Institute's Russ Hudson and Gayle Scott and trained in Andrea Isaacs' Enneamotion.

About the Illustrator

Doug Meffert is a freelance cartoonist and gag writer residing in New Orleans, Louisiana. Doug's cartoons have appeared in a variety of print and digital media comic strips, including King Features Syndicate, The Funny Times Newspaper, and Recycled Paper Greetings, as well as other commercial cartoon/graphic projects.